RIGHTS RESERVED

- Focus on the Children.

Our church has not met regularly for about a year.

I've been making breakfast (bacon and scrambled eggs) while watching the livestream, and it's been pretty fun. In a matter of seconds, I can return to the coffee pot and re-fill my cup. In addition, it's not ear-splittingly loud.

And since we've kept up our regular meetings,
I've been fine. It's been fine; I miss some aspects of Sunday morning church, but not too much.

But the thing I've regretted the most is missing out on family trips. Our high school-aged
daughter's inability to help with the 3-year-olds
is something I've missed. I wish the middle schooler's little group still met in person

because I miss seeing everyone. Their
spiritual lives have been greatly aided
by attending
services and small groups, but
recently, that hasn't been
the case.

It's a common sentiment shared by
many. The involvement of adults in the
church has always been fueled by the
involvement of their children.

That's why, when you're ready to ask
everyone back in a significant way, the
kids should be at
the center of your message. Use
language that stresses the value of
children interacting with
caring adults in small groups.
Relationships that have been
neglected for too long should be
prioritized.

Ministry Spark's Andrew Brown
warns, "You cannot afford to not have
an option for families when you
reopen."

Yes, Andrew is correct, but I'd go even
further.
Even if it means cutting back on content
   aimed at adults, you should
   concentrate on familyfriendly
   solutions.

Some churches are only reopening
   their student and children's areas,
   maximizing their **facilities to create
   additional physical separation.**

MEDITATIVE NOTES

- Pay more attention to the people than the material

According to the results of a recent Gallop Study, the mental health of Americans is at an all-time low.

Almost everyone feels worse about their situation now than they did this time last year. With a nine-point decline from last year to this one, it is at its worst in the past two decades.

Only one group seeing improvement?

Weekly worshippers are those who actively participate in religious activities.

Take a moment to let that sink in.

The male gender reports worse outcomes.

Women report feeling even less successful.

Conservatives report worse mental health than liberals.

The Democratic Party agrees.

Income and marital status are recorded.

However, weekly churchgoers get a +4 bonus.

I think the social element of religious services is a contributing factor. Church is more than a place to worship; it is a community of worshippers. We don't just pray in church; we pray with one another.

When inviting people back to church, it's the relationships you build with them that will have the most impact.

Those are the pieces that have been lacking up until now. That's exactly what the public wants.

Try saying something like, "we can't wait to see you face to face" or "we've missed you." Work hard but make time for developing real relationships with others.

Far too many religious institutions are preoccupied with what is spoken and sung during services. That's fantastic! However, these experiences may be had digitally with minimal loss in quality. Videoconferencing may be the most effective way to spend 30 minutes of your time listening to someone talk. We've gotten fairly proficient at digesting web information over the past few months.

MEDITATIVE NOTES

- community is unique.

It's never quite good enough, no matter how many Zoom or FaceTime calls we make. When Christians get together, something miraculous happens.

Take advantage of this by centering your regathering strategy on the individuals, rather than the processes.

Some folks, your die-hard supporters, will be waiting outside the doors when you're ready to begin assembling.

However, much more work is needed to win over the general public.

Sending out a few emails and making a few social media posts over the course of two weeks won't cut it.

All aspects of the reopening, from safety measures to motivation, need to be addressed in a comprehensive communication strategy. And the timeframe for this strategy should be at least six months.

Here are some things to keep in mind as you put together your strategy for communication.

Prioritize email but don't neglect the other channels. I trust that you've been actively collecting email addresses over the past few months. This may be the dullest method of communication, but it gets the job done. You have control over the people who hear your message, and technology won't be the deciding factor. Plan out a whole email series, with each message addressing a different perspective.

After that, you may add things like video, member testimonies, and more to your social media platforms. Every strategy and medium is a tool in your arsenal. They're all necessary, yet each has a certain function. The plan can hardly be overbuilt.

MEDITATIVE NOTES

- Stop trying to guilt them into it and start encouraging them instead.

To feel guilty is to feel demotivated. It's disheartening. That's paralyzing.

Encouragement, hope, and compassionate understanding are what will truly drive change in people.

We should avoid guilting others in two common ways:

Don't make them feel bad about skipping it.

If they want to view it online, let them.

There's no need to frown upon folks tuning in to a church service online. We would not provide
them with a choice if one were available.

During the pandemic, most of us relied heavily on our online church. People in the church I lead have been making decisions to follow Jesus and joining our family for months before they set foot in the building.

Guilt-tripping viewers into not using your live streaming service is not only ineffective, but also hypocritical. Instead, you should be thankful that they chose to watch your service out of all the available options (both religious and secular).

MEDITATIVE NOTES

- Do something for them that
they can't do for themselves
online.

Rather than just watching it online, why should someone travel to your church? The answer to that query should be powerful and self-evident. To you and everyone else there as well.

No one attending a physical church service should ever ask themselves, "Why did I come today?" I could have easily found all that information online.

This is the test that every church must face today. You should provide the finest possible online church service while also making the inperson experience captivating enough that everyone who sees will want to attend.

So, what advantages does traditional worship have over virtual worship?

Adds a human dimension

Social gatherings for sharing and learning
Strengthening bonds

The atmosphere of private worship as we lift
our voices in song

Communion with one another at the Lord's
table

Plus a whole lot more.

Is there a pattern you can pick out among the things on the list? What makes going to church in person so unique is what doesn't make it onto the stage or into the video.

To make the most of our time spent together in church in the future years, we must work to improve our interpersonal skills.

Some of these can be accomplished online, but even the most comprehensive live broadcast will only give you a taste of what's going on backstage.

MEDITATIVE NOTES

- Try to contact them.

If so, who have you missed? Just tell them.

Not in an attempt to make you feel bad (go back to points 1 and 2), but to express how much you are missed." way.

A few weeks ago, I urged those of you who were able to attend our in-person meeting to take a look around and think to yourself, "Who haven't I seen in a while?"To do so, pick up the phone and say, "Hi!"

Since then, I've received other accounts of how encouraging and healing those phone calls and texts were for absent church members.

MEDITATIVE NOTES

- Make amends if necessary.

There was no perfect church in the face of the pandemic. Every one of us has made blunders and forgotten someone important. Those omissions should generally be filed under "we did what we could with what we knew."

A formal apology may be necessary, though, if we have seriously offended someone. As a matter of fact, I've done something similar before. In each case, it also served to repair the damage done to the relationship.

MEDITATIVE NOTES

- Inspiring a closer walk with Jesus in the here and now

Helping people maintain a personal relationship with Jesus Christ is of infinitely greater value than getting them back into the church building.

It can feel like a sales job sometimes when we're trying to convince people to attend church, especially if you're the pastor. But if we're helping them grow in their relationship with Jesus whether or not they show up, they'll know we're not interested in getting anything out of it for ourselves.

Check out my latest essay, "Will The Congregation Come Back? " for more information on this.Not Something We Need to Be Overly Worried About" (6 Alternative Queries).

MEDITATIVE NOTES

Made in the USA
Middletown, DE
18 October 2023

41021894R00020